Mouse's Summer Muddle

Anita Loughrey
and Daniel Howarth

QED Publishing

Mouse dashed past the old apple tree. The sun was high in the sky. Colourful flowers speckled the grass.

This book belongs to:

....

Consultant: Barbara Taylor
Editor: Lauren Taylor
Designer: Elaine Wilkinson

Copyright © QED Publishing 2012

First published in the UK in 2012 by
QED Publishing
A Quarto Group company
230 City Road
London EC1V 2TT

www.qed-publishing.co.uk

A catalogue record for this book is available from the British Library.

ISBN 978 1 84835 817 1

Printed in China

"What a beautiful summer's day!"
said Mouse.

Two butterflies chased each
other in the warm summer breeze.

Mouse followed them
to the pond.

She saw something sparkling in the water.
"What's that?" asked Mouse.

Rabbit was playing by the pond.
"Look, Rabbit!" said Mouse.
"Something is sparkling!"

"Maybe there's treasure at the bottom!"
cried Rabbit, and hopped off into the wood.

Frog was sitting on a lily pad.
"Will you fetch the treasure from the
bottom of the pond?" asked Mouse.

"Of course!" said Frog.
And he dived into the water.

Mouse waited...

...and waited...

...and waited.

Busy bees collected
nectar from
the flowers.

A dragonfly
whizzed past.

Ants marched
to their nest.
But there was still
no sign of Frog.

Frog finally leapt out of the
pond with a splash.
"There's no treasure down there!"
he croaked.

Mouse was puzzled.
What was sparkling in the pond, then?

Mouse was about to
give up when Owl
flew down to the
water's edge.

"There's something sparkling
in the pond," Mouse said to Owl.

Owl glanced down at the pond and then up at the clear blue sky.

"Move closer to the water and look in,"
said Owl. "What do you see now?"

Mouse peered over the edge of the pond.
She saw her own face staring back at her.

"I can see myself, of course!"
said Mouse.

"You can see the sun's reflection too," said Owl.

Mouse looked up at the bright sun in the sky, and then at the sparkles on the pond.

Now she understood
her muddle.

"It's just the sun's reflection on the
water," said Mouse. "Thank you, Owl!"

Summer activities

Fun and simple ideas for you and
your child to explore together.

Make a flower collage. Using
brightly coloured paper or
card, cut out flower shapes
and glue them to long green paper
stalks. Make a cone shape from a sheet
of card, then pop the flowers in at the
top, where the flowers on a real bouquet
would be. This colourful collage will
brighten up any room!

How many insects can you spot?
Visit your local library to
borrow a book that shows
pictures of common insects. Ask
your child to look closely at the
pictures and then see if he
or she can spot any of the
insects outside.

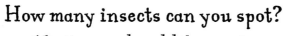

Make a butterfly painting. Take a piece of thick paper and fold it in half. Unfold it, then paint one half of a butterfly on one half of the paper, going right up to the crease in the middle. While the paint is still wet, fold the paper in half again and press down so that the butterfly prints on the other half of the paper. You could cut it out and hang it on your child's bedroom wall.

Act out the story with your child. Use paper, pens, pencils and paints to make masks of Mouse and her friends. Can your child remember anything the characters said? Does your child want to act out the story as it is in the book, or do they want to change the story in their own way?

What did we learn about summer?

It is a beautiful summer's day. Summer is usually a hot season. The sun is strong at this time of year because the part of the Earth where it is summer is turned towards the sun. Sunscreen helps to block out the harmful rays of the sun and stops you getting sunburnt.

Bees are collecting nectar from the flowers. Summer is a good time to watch insects munching leaves or sucking the sweet nectar from flowers. Butterflies drink nectar through a long feeding tube which works rather like a straw. Bees turn nectar from flowers into honey, which they feed to their young.

Mouse sees a dragonfly whizzing past. Dragonflies are hunters, which scoop up flying insects with their spiky legs. They can hover, dart forwards and backwards, and stop suddenly. Dragonflies can fly at speeds of up to 60 kilometres per hour.

Frog dives into the pond to help Mouse. Frogs are excellent swimmers. They use their long, powerful back legs and flipper-like feet to push through the water. Frogs can breathe air through their lungs, but underwater they breathe through their skin.

Mouse sees the sun's reflection in the pond. Reflections happen because light bounces back from surfaces. Smooth, flat surfaces (such as the surface of a pond) produce the best reflections because most of the light is reflected back in one direction.